# It's In The Bag

### Kimberly Gordon

Energion Publications
Gonzalez, Florida
2012

Cover Design: Henry Neufeld

ISBN10: 1-893729-67-2
ISBN13: 978-1-893729-67-4


Energion Publications
P.O. Box 841
Gonzalez, FL  32560
www.energionpubs.com

# Contents

Introduction ........................................................................ 1

1    Makeup ....................................................................... 3

2    A Good Foundation .................................................... 5

3    Lipstick ...................................................................... 7

4    Mascara ..................................................................... 9

5    Rouge/Blush ........................................................... 12

6    Mirror ...................................................................... 14

7    Highlighter Pen ....................................................... 16

8    Candy ....................................................................... 19

9    Brush/Comb ........................................................... 20

10   Band-Aids ............................................................... 22

11   Tissues ...................................................................... 24

12   Crumbs ..................................................................... 26

13   "Son" Glasses ........................................................... 28

14   Cell Phone ................................................................ 30

15   Keys .......................................................................... 32

16   Hand Cream ............................................................. 34

17   Debit Card – What's in Your Wallet? ..................... 36

Conclusion .......................................................................... 38

Thank you to my friends
Julie Tidwell and Rhonda Ford
for all their help with the study questions

# Introduction

Years ago, there was a cartoon cat named Felix. He got himself into all sorts of jams and tight spots, but he carried a bag that was full of tools or whatever he needed to get out of trouble. I remember the little song that went with his show. "Felix the cat, the wonderful, wonderful cat, whenever he is in a fix, he'll reach into his bag of tricks!" It was a fun cartoon, but his little bag was key to saving the day. Wouldn't it be nice if we could have a bag like that? Whatever we needed would be in there to fix whatever comes our way each day. Where do I get one?

Actually though, we do have our "tool bag" of things that we need. We carry our purses everywhere. I don't leave home without mine and I panic if it's missing. My purse is a part of me, even though I change it out every season. Now, imagine if we, as women of God, were given a purse by Christ himself. A gift, a handbag, full of everything we needed to get through each day with every season of life. Awesome! If heaven's angels handed them out in all the best department stores, can you imagine the line? Oh my goodness! It would make the news for sure. "Handbags from Jesus, given out today at department stores across the country to every woman who believes in Him. Free gifts inside ..."

What would they look like? What would be in it? Would the outside be smooth, black leather, macrame, pink fur, feathers, or plastic? It would be as unique as we are for certain. It might be gold and covered with rubies and others precious gemstones. Maybe the rubies would be inside to remind me how much I am worth to Him.

> For who can find a virtuous woman? For her price is far above rubies. — Proverbs 31:10

Far above rubies? I like the sound of that. Sounds out of my price range though. Only one entity in all of creation can afford something truly priceless and that would be our heavenly Father. We are priceless to Him. Hallelujah!

So let's determine what might be inside our purse from heaven. Let's take a peek inside. Oooohhhh. I see lipstick, mascara, foundation ... we get make up. Yahoo! There are band-aids, a mirror, a comb, a cell phone .... I know what you are thinking. Gee, that's nothing special. All that stuff is in my purse right now. What makes this purse so special? Let's use God's word, and find out.

## GROUP ACTIVITY: PURSE SCAVENGER HUNT

Ask the ladies to pull out their purses. When you call out an item, they dig into their purse and find it, and earn a point for each item. Winner at the end has the most points.

Band-aid
Comb/brush
Lipstick
Mirror
Mascara
Pen
Tissues (clean or not)
Candy (including gum, tic-tacs, anything)
Sunglasses
Nail Polish
Straw
Paper clip
Cell Phone
Receipt

Tie breaker: what's the weirdest thing in your purse? The group votes on the winner.

# 1
## Makeup

I just love Looney Toons. I grew up on those cartoons in the 70's. I'll even admit I still watch them today, from time to time. There was one particular story line where one of the characters shouts "Makeup!" Of course, the poor shmuck sitting in the chair gets a face full of powder. I don't think our makeup from Jesus is quite so surprising. The word "makeup" in itself has scriptural ties. The makeup of someone is who they are, what they are. Is your makeup good or bad today? Are you sugar and spice and everything nice, or sour lemons? Your makeup is your countenance. How you hold and present yourself, how you interact with other people, and so on. Ladies, if we are saved through Christ, then our "makeup" should be holy, for He is holy and He is in us. Do people see Him in you? Are you "madeup" of Christ?

Romans 8:10 tells us, "But if Christ is in you ... the Spirit gives life because of righteousness ...." And Galatians 2:20 says, "I have been crucified with Christ and I no longer live, but Christ lives in me."

So if Christ is in us, shouldn't we let Him be in control? He is going to give us a better attitude that we could have on our own. For example, what if you stub your toe on the coffee table and your children are watching. How do you react? What do you say?

What if you hit every single red light all the way to work? (Been there, done that – and I was ready to kill someone by the time I finally got to my desk.) What if your children are fighting at the breakfast table and it's not even 7 AM yet. (Been there, done that too.) When you get in these stressful situations, how do you react? Like Christ? Or in the flesh?

What a difference when we do things in the flesh. In the Bible, your attitude is described as your countenance. As women of God,

3

our countenance should shine light. Let Him be your "makeup" that makes you shine each and every day. Psalm 4:6 reads, "Let the light of your face shine on us." Proverbs 15:13 tells us that "A merry heart makes a cheerful countenance." And Psalm 42:11 says "Hope in God ... who is the health of my countenance."

These are wonderful passages of scripture to get us through the day with reminders of how we should behave.

## GROUP DISCUSSION:

1. What are some situations that you've been in where you acted in the flesh and not in the spirit?

2. Can you think of a time when you did act righteously, when your "makeup" was pleasing to Christ?

3. Are you conscious that someone is almost always watching you? Do you have good behavior testimony? Are you setting a good example for others?

# 2
## A Good Foundation

Every woman that sells makeup knows that besides great skin, which very few of us actually have, you need to start with the right kind of foundation. It is the base, the bottom layer, the thing that gives us a sturdy platform on which to build. What kind of foundation are you using? I don't mean a name brand, I mean what do you base your life on? I am telling you now, let your foundation be Jesus Christ.

Luke 6:48-49 reads,

"He is like a man building a house, who dug down deep and laid the foundation on rock. When a flood came, the torrent struck that house but could not shake it, because it was well built. 49 But the one who hears my words and does not put them into practice is like a man who built a house on the ground without a foundation. The moment the torrent struck that house, it collapsed and its destruction was complete."

If your foundation is anything else, throw it out, it's no good. Throw away those old notions and misconceived ideas you got from that beauty magazine. Throw out those hateful words said at home or by kids at school. Throw out feelings of doubt and poor self-worth brought on by society. Let Christ tell you how to live. He wants to be your foundation.

Nevertheless, God's solid foundation stands firm ....
"The Lord knows those who are his ...."
— 2 Timothy 2:19

He knows me! He knows you!

By the grace God has given me, I laid a foundation as a wise builder, and someone else is building on it. But each one should build with care. For no one can lay any foundation other than the one already laid, which is Jesus Christ. — 1 Corinthians 3:10-11

Hallelujah, Amen!

Inside this wonderful heavenly purse, we have foundation, but no concealer. Yikes! "I need concealer," you are telling me. "I have blemishes." Yes, we all do, but can you see where I'm going with this? You cannot hide anything from the Lord. He knows all, sees all. You cannot cover up anything, not even little secrets. Two things will come of this.

1. Because he is watching this blemish, he is waiting for you to confess it. Come clean. Ask for forgiveness. Refer to these scriptures for confirmation: Proverbs 28:13, 1 John 1:9, Psalm 32:5.

2. Because we don't have concealer, we must really not need it. Once we are saved by grace though faith, we are spotless, blemish free. Jesus paid the price for our sins. When we accept Him as Savior, he cleanses us. God now only sees us as pure.

... and the blood of Jesus his Son purifies us from all sin. — 1 John 1:7

You are already clean because of the word I have spoken to you. — John 15:3

Gotta love that good news scripture!

Here's a few more if you want to look them up: 1 John 3:3 and Revelation 19:7-8. Clean white and righteous. That's what I want to be for my Lord. How about you?

## GROUP DISCUSSION:

1. Can you name some other things that we might base our life on?

2. Don't share, but think about any secret "blemish" that you might have. Are you sure it's a secret? Has it affected any other areas of your life? Can you work on it?

3. Is your "foundation" firm? Is it solidified?

# 3
## *Lipstick*

My husband hates lipstick, but I like it. It gives my face color and makes my lips pretty. At least, I think so. But a lipstick from Jesus, what would that be like? The color really doesn't matter, you could use your favorite. The important thing is, does it make your mouth pretty? I don't mean vain pretty, I mean, does it give you a beautiful mouth?

Do you ever yell, swear or complain? Or do you praise, comfort, smile, witness, edify, and forgive? I am guilty of not always having a beautiful mouth. Only with God's lipstick can we continually remember his word.

I said, "I will watch my ways and keep my tongue from sin; I will put a muzzle on my mouth ..." — Psalm 39:1

She speaks with wisdom, and faithful instruction is on her tongue. — Proverbs 31:26

Those that guard their lips preserve their life, but those who speak rashly will come to ruin. — Proverbs 12:3

Keep your mouth free of perversity, keep corrupt talk from your lips. — Proverbs 4:24

Your mouth has the power to build up or tear down. Make sure each day, when you put on your lipstick, that you put on a beautiful mouth as well.

## GROUP DISCUSSION:

1. Have you cussed today? This week?

2. Do you complain and whine a lot?

3.  Have you blessed anyone with your words today? List some ways we can bless others with words.

4.  Does your mouth have any bad or good habits?

Leader idea: Print up scripture from this section in the Bible study, or any other of your favorites from the Bible regarding speech. Cut them out for everyone and ask the ladies to tape scripture to their lipstick tubes as a daily reminder to use their mouths for good.

# 4
## *Mascara*

Just as lipstick reminds us to have a pretty mouth, mascara can remind us that we must be careful with our eyes. The danger here is twofold. We must guard what we see and how we see. 1 John 2:16 talks about the lust of the eyes. Do your eyes ever want anything? We want what we see in Sunday's ads or on TV. We want that house or that car or that man!

Death and destruction are never satisfied, and neither are human eyes. — Proverbs 27:20

I challenge you to go one week without wanting something that your eyes see. It could be something as simple as a piece of cake. We see it, the body reacts, and then our brain tells us, "Go get that cake." And that's just cake. I used it as an example, but many times, what the eyes see, the body wants. So guard yourself from worldly wanting and be thankful for what you already have.

Also with our eyes, we take in sinful sights. Watching TV has become a dangerous pastime. It is so full of worldly visions and sinful behavior. I can't stand it. In fact, if I lived alone, I wouldn't even own a television. When you watch TV, do you have to send your children out of the room? Is there a show you love that you would never watch with your parents over? When you watch TV, think about Christ sitting next to you sharing your bowl of snacks. "Um, Jesus, would you pass the Chex mix please?" If you still feel good about the program, then by all means, enjoy. But if you have any doubts about being entertained by violence or smut, or whatever is on that rectangular screen, maybe you should change the channel. And quite frankly, it is certainly OK to TURN IT OFF!

I will not look with approval on anything that is vile. — Psalm 101:3

Not everything we do with our eyes is bad though. Of course it isn't. We just have to use them wisely. If we look at people with

God's light and in His perspective, we will see them differently. We will see the inner person, not the outer.

The Lord does not look at the things human beings look at.

... People look at the outward appearance, but the Lord looks at the heart. — 1 Samuel 16:7

You've heard the saying, never judge a book by its cover. This is never judge a person by their appearance. And how often do we do this when we see homeless people, or teenage mothers, or a person from a certain race, creed, size or color. You fill in the blank. There is always someone in the world you are judging.

... to open eyes that are blind. — Isaiah 42:7

Woe to those who are wise in their own eyes and clever in their own sight. — Isaiah 5:21

If you see people like Christ sees them, as a soul worth saving, it changes things. Every person becomes special and worth knowing. I'm not saying we are going to get along with every person. Some people are very difficult to be around. And some people are dangerous, so use common sense. But if we don't judge, and approach each new person as a friend, we open up a whole new world of possibilities. You can make a new friend every day. And believe me, we live in a very lonely world. Nearly every woman I know could use a few more real friends.

We can also use our eyes to enjoy the beauty and wonder of the world He created. There are so many marvelous places and things to see. Even just a sky full of clouds can bring wonder and peace to your heart and mind. A rose makes you smile. A baby makes you smile. A silly puppy brings joy. Never underestimate the power of a pleasant, happy moment. Share it with a friend.

We also use our eyes to read and study our Bibles. Bringing His word into our mind, heart and soul brings life-saving power.

The commands of the Lord are radiant, giving light to the eyes. — Psalm 19:8

Keep yours clean and bright, and use your heavenly mascara to put on Christ's eyes. Use them to really "see."

To conclude this section, I will close with scripture from Matthew 6:22-23:

The eye is the lamp of the body. If your eyes are healthy, your whole body will be full of light. But if your eyes are unhealthy, your whole body will be full of darkness. If then the light with in you is darkness, how great is that darkness!

## GROUP DISCUSSION:

1. Can you think of a time when you saw something and said, "Ooh, I *want* that," even though you didn't *need* it?

2. What shows do you watch that might be questionable? Why are they questionable? Are you really thinking about what you're taking into your mind, heart and home. What are your children watching?

3. I challenge you all to have a NO TV day each week. See how it impacts your family and peace of mind. Use the time wisely, play a game, take a walk, talk.

4. When we see someone, do we judge unfairly? Are we prejudiced against certain groups of people? Ex. Teenagers, homeless, old, etc.

5. Do you compare yourself to other women, either at work, church, or in magazines? My young friend Gabrielle Ford offered me the best quote: "Be Yourself! Everyone else is taken."

# 5
## *Rouge/Blush*

When our cheeks turn pink naturally, it means we are blushing. When we get embarrassed about something, we blush. I believe rouge in our purse from Jesus means that we need to be more embarrassed about certain things. Maybe He wants to remind us to be modest, it's a dying virtue. Sometimes I wonder where all the true ladies have gone. 1 Timothy 2:9 says,

> I also want the women to dress modestly, with decency and propriety ...

As Christian women, we need to police ourselves. Who hasn't walked through church and seen a woman's blouse so low that half her chest is hanging out? I'm embarrassed and it's not even mine. What signals are we putting out when our clothing doesn't fit properly? Are we telling God that we don't care what the Bible says? Ladies, please, have some decency and cover up. Leave cleavage in the bedroom; there is a time and place for it, but not in public.

There are lots of beautiful clothes that don't let "the girls" peep out. I enjoy shopping as much as most women, but I don't gravitate toward the too low, too thin, too tight pieces on the rack. I challenge you to walk through the mall and count how many women have too much flesh showing. I live in Florida, so my numbers might be higher than yours; it does get horribly hot here, but there are tank tops that fit decently if you look for them.

It is better that we clothe ourselves with strength and dignity (Proverbs 31:25). We keep our self-respect in the process. And for all the young women of God reading this text, please watch your hemlines. I've seen teenagers at church pulling down their dresses once they sat down because their undergarments were about to show. Good grief! If a dress or skirt is that short, you shouldn't be in it! It's lingerie at that point! Your body is God's temple.

Protect it.

Then out came a woman to meet him, dressed like a prostitute ... — Proverbs 7:10

What I wear, matters! What I wear, matters! Tell yourself that every day. Back in Bible days, appearance mattered, and it still does. People will judge you based on your clothing. You may have the best testimony in the room, but if parts of you are hanging out, the distraction will detract from the message. I'm not talking about expensive clothes, those are not necessary. But clothes that fit ALL of you properly are more important than you realize.

Take time to respect yourself, then use your blush, and keep your modesty in check.

## GROUP DISCUSSION

1. Our clothing represents us, we are our own walking advertisement. What do your clothes say about you? Are you giving the right message?

2. Are there any modesty issues that need to be addressed within the church/group?

3. Do you have an article of clothing that should be thrown out or saved for wearing only at home?

4. Where do you shop? Where do you take your children to shop? Are there any stores in your area that should be avoided altogether? Why?

5. Discuss the media/marketing deluge to turn our young daughters into adult women. How can we build a wall of protection around them? What steps can we take to ensure their modesty?

# 6
## Mirror

Mirror, mirror on the wall...uh...in my purse... Who's the holiest of them all? Christ Jesus of course! When you look in the mirror, who do you honestly see? Who are you reflecting?

In Genesis, chapter 1, verses 26 and 27 it tells us:

> Then God said, "Let us make mankind in our image, in our likeness. ..." So God created mankind in his own image, in the image of God he created them; male and female he created them.

So from the very beginning, we are the image of God the Father, God the Son and the Holy Spirit. Do your friends see Him in you? Does your family see Him in you? Do you see Him in you? We can be grouchy as all get out on Sunday morning while we are trying to get everyone fed and dressed for church on time. You may grumble in the car all the way there at traffic or dumb drivers or the state of the nation. But the moment you get to church, you put on your "Christian" face. You smile. When people ask how you are, you say, "Fine." Your poor family took the brunt of your not so holy image all morning. You show a different face in public.

Let us be careful to manage ourselves more evenly and reflect God to everyone.

> And just as we have borne the image of the earthly man, so shall we bear the image of the heavenly man.
> — 1 Corinthians 15:49

Are you a heavenly woman? You can be. It just takes patience and practice. Every time you look in a mirror, remember that you are what you see.

# GROUP DISCUSSION:

1.  Your countenance goes beyond your face. It starts in the heart and mind. Who are you really? Can you make a short list of qualities you reflect? For a real eye opener, have a friend make a list for you, and do the same for her. Be nice, but be honest.

2.  Do you fake your happiness and put on a "good" face?

3.  Do you need a mirror make-over? If you could change one thing about your countenance, what would it be? Is there something you need to "clean-out"? Some examples might be: not forgiving someone, holding on to bitterness, hate, not letting go of sorrow, feeling sorry for yourself, etc. Can you think of others?

4.  Read 2 Corinthians 3:18. Are you being transformed into his image with ever increasing glory?

5.  Read 1 Corinthians 13:12. One day we will look upon the face of Christ in person. Until then, we can only reflect His image. Be proud of who you are. He made you! How can you shine His glory for others to see? Remember, that to put yourself down, is to criticize His creation.

# 7
## Highlighter Pen

My husband used to work for a company that gave out highlighter pens at conferences. I would take a few from his box before he left, because these pens were awesome. I kept one in my Bible at all times so I could not only take notes in church, but also highlight scripture as I went along. My Bible is very colorful on the inside, but it lets me know where I've been.

Maybe, since there is a highlighter pen in our purse from Jesus, he wants us to use it to know His word.

Scripture tells us in Joshua 1:8:

Keep this book of the Law always on your lips; meditate on it day and night, so that you may be careful to do everything written in it. Then you will be prosperous and successful.

Gosh, that's a nice blessing. Prosperous and successful? Who wouldn't want that? Another great passage in Deuteronomy 6:6-9 reads:

These commandments that I give you today are to be on your hearts. Impress them on your children. Talk about them when you sit at home and when you walk along the road, when you lie down and when you get up. Tie them as symbols on your hands and bind them on your foreheads. Write them on the doorframes of your houses and on your gates.

Where I come from, we say "That will preach!" If we have something on our hearts, then it's dear to us. We think about it, often. If that's not a hint, then I don't know what is. I have an old dictionary (American Heritage) from 1969 that my grandmother and her mother used when they played Scrabble. The women from my family are big on Scrabble. But in this dictionary, the third and fourth definitions of the word "impress" read as follows: To produce a vivid perception or image of, To affect or influence deeply... When we teach children, we are to impress them. If someone is impressive, then they are awesome in our eyes, they command our attention and respect. How much more so is our God? We MUST tell our children how awesome he is. We must train them so that he influences their lives. This is not optional. If we are Christians, we must.

We are also told to talk about them at home and when we are out. Do you fellowship with other Christians and talk about scripture? I can say, some of my best, deepest conversations have been about the Word. And when you talk and listen and share, you learn.

Duh. That's the point! I do caution you on this though. I know a very Godly woman who posts several times a day on Facebook. All she puts on there is scripture or passages in hymns. This isn't wrong, but does she not have a voice? If friends are talking about a baby shower, don't walk up and start quoting scripture. Just talk. There is a time and place for everything, and if you're a walking Bible, you might annoy some people. Just saying ...

Do we mull over scripture at night when we go to bed and pick it up again the next morning? Actually, that is what we are told to do, and if you do your daily devotions at night or in the morning, this comes easy. And tying them on our hands? How about jewelry? There are lots of pretty passages imprinted on bracelets and such. Why not get one? I have a friend who has WWJD earrings. They are great conversation starters. Putting them on our houses is easy now too, with so much scripture on artwork. These just become daily reminders of His love to us. I even have a two by two tapestry hanging in my kitchen with Home Rules on it. It lists twelve awesome scriptures on how we are to treat one another within the family. Awesome!

But who delight in the law of the Lord and meditate on his law day and night. They are like a tree planted by streams of water which yields its fruit in season and

17

whose leaf does not wither – whatever they do prospers.
— Psalm 1:2-3

... This law of the Lord is to be on your lips.
— Exodus 13:9

Do you think, that if He wants us to think about scripture day and night, write it in our homes, on our gates, between our eyes, on our hands, and talk about it continually, that He's trying to tell us something? He wants us to KNOW IT! So what better way than to study our Bibles, memorize scripture, take notes in church, underline passages, highlight chapters, whatever it takes.

## GROUP DISCUSSION:

1. Do you have Scripture in your home? What kind?

2. Do you talk with your children about God's word, or do you leave it up to the church to train them?

3. Highlighted Scripture brings out the word and leaves a trail of where you've been. What do your Bible pages say about you? Do your Scripture pages remind you of a time when God spoke to you?

4. What is your favorite verse? Why?

# 8

## Candy

Horray! Make mine chocolate. Chocolate makes me happy. With candy in our purse, the Lord wants to remind us that his love and his words are sweet. We should be happy with his fat free, calorie free, pure good sweetness!

How sweet are your words to my taste, sweeter than honey to my mouth. — Psalm 119:103

Happy is the people, whose god is the Lord. — Psalm 144:15

When one of my daughters was a toddler, she used to walk around and say, "Happy, happy!" I always knew then that she was in a good mood. This reminds me now of the sweetness of Jesus. He makes us happy, happy.

Whoever trusts in the Lord, happy is he. — Proverbs 16:20 (NKJV)

Gracious words are a honeycomb, sweet to the soul ... — Proverbs 16:24

My daughters are about to turn sixteen and I ordered a small chocolate fountain for their birthday party. We can't wait to use it, because we know it's going to be wonderful, delectable, heavenly, yummy. But honestly, I know it doesn't compare to the sweet love of Jesus. He's a truffle from heaven. (Sorry, no offense.) So next time you reach for a piece of candy, remember how sweet He is.

## GROUP DISCUSSION:

1. Do you make time to enjoy and savor your "candy" time with Jesus? If not, what can you do to change that?

2. Most of us look forward to eating chocolate. Do you crave God the same way?

# 9
## *Brush/Comb*

"Oh what a tangled web we weave, when first we practice to deceive" (Sir Walter Scott). Ever heard of that phrase? And it's true. We sure can get ourselves in a heap of trouble in this world, especially if we try to solve all of life's problems ourselves. Thank goodness God equips us with a comb and brush in our beautiful purse to smooth out the knots and tangles of life.

Better a dry crust with peace and quiet than a house full of feasting and strife. — Proverbs 17:1

Amen to that one! I once had so much strife in my home, I jumped in my car and drove out of my state and through two more! I cried for nine hours that day, but by the time I got home, God had taken off the pressure and I felt so much better.

Mortals, born of woman, are of few days and full of trouble. — Job 14:1

Ever known a toddler, a teenager, a drama queen, or a man? Need I say more?

The Lord is a refuge for the oppressed, a stronghold in times of trouble. — Psalm 9:9

Praise God for this one, literally. I can't tell you how many times he was the only one I could go to when I needed someone to comfort me. On my knees in my closet I cried out to him for help. He saw me through. He will do the same for you.

Throughout the tribes of Israel, all the people were arguing ... — 2 Samuel 19:9

Gosh, did someone set up a secret camera in my house? Can't we all just get along? You know why we can't? Sin and selfishness. It all comes down to that.

Such tangles and knots and trouble. So much of it daily, but how much do we honestly give to the Lord? When we fix it, things can only get worse. We muddle things up. Trust Him to work out those tangles in life. Sometimes the brush hurts, but it gets the job done.

## GROUP DISCUSSION:

1.  Is anyone willing to share a story about how God untangled a mess in your life?

2.  Close your eyes and imagine that someone is brushing your hair. It's relaxing, right? When God brushes our hair, he is taking care of our lives. He helps us maintain the lustre and shine when we spend this time with him. If we are disobedient, He has to get out the comb to remove the knots. Knots hurt, so clean your brushes today and thank Jesus for smoothing things out. Pray about any knots that are hurting you.

# 10
## Band-Aids

I am stuck on Band-Aid brand, 'cause ... (can you finish this?) Most of you probably remember that jingle from old commercials. I have amazing news for you. There's a bandage even better – the Jesus brand. He is our healer and restorer, both physically and emotionally.

In the back of one of my Bibles at home, there are fifty-five (55) references to the words heal, healing and health. That's a lot!

If you try to think of a list of things that hurt, it's not hard. Injury, illness, depression, grief, deceit, disappointment, failure, rejection, distress, misfortune, regret, sorrow, injustice, despair, suffering, insult, evil, strife, death, lies, disaster, meanness, cruelty, the list goes on...

Matthew 9:12 tells us: "... Jesus said, 'It is not the healthy who need a doctor, but the sick.'"

Just a few verses later, in Matthew 9:22, Jesus heals a woman with these words: "'Take heart daughter,' he said, 'your faith has healed you.' And the woman was healed from that moment." Of course he doesn't heal everyone from everything, we've all lost a loved one to cancer or some other ailment. But he does heal, he just works on a much bigger plan than we do. We are one pixel on a TV screen as big as the universe!

He is our ultimate, almighty healer. Several years ago my husband went through a bad bout with depression. It lasted for weeks and the doctors prescribed medication that was not working. He slept through days at a time, lost twenty pounds and was a shell of his former self.

At my wits end, I cried out to God to heal him. I did this all day on a Thursday with fasting and prayer. On Friday, my husband woke up, got up, and was 90% back to his old self. He went off the medicine cold turkey! Coincidence? I don't think so. God healed him! It was an amazing miracle and now I can share it with you. I sometimes wonder now if my husband was put through this so I would get to where God wanted ME to be.

"Heal me Lord," lies within Psalm 6:2. What a wonderful prayer this is and don't you know it makes Christ smile when we lean on him? My husband has since continued to struggle with depression and we have learned it runs in the family. He takes medication to help him with this biological problem, but I still pray for him on a regular basis. Are you praying for the ones you love? It certainly can't hurt to ask God for healing.

## GROUP DISCUSSION:

1. Does anyone have a story they can share about a time when God healed you or a loved one?

2. If you have a wound and don't protect it, it can get infected. Jesus can soothe and protect us if we are patient. Have you ever ripped your band aid off too soon? What happened?

# *Tissues*

Tissues. My mother has enough of these stuck in purses and pockets and jackets to fill a kitchen sink! I suppose she just wants to be prepared. Christ is the same way. He is prepared to share our pain and sorrow.

In the King James version, Job 14:22 says, "But his flesh upon him shall have pain, and his soul within him shall mourn." This ties in a lot with our last subject of band-aids. We have all experienced pain and helped other friends through it. Thankfully, we have a loving God who shows us sympathy and care. We go through these trials and seasons for a reason, but we are not alone. "Jesus wept." *John 11:35* is the shortest verse in the Bible. Isn't it comforting to know that He feels our pain too? He knows what it is like to be so overwhelmed emotionally that you have to cry to get it out. Can you imagine touching His face to wipe His tears? He does the same for us. We don't cry alone. He is always there.

... and the Lord God will wipe away tears from off all faces. — Isaiah 25:8

Those who sow in tears shall reap with songs of joy. — Psalm 126:5

So let your tears fall. God will wipe them away and put a song of gladness in your heart.

## GROUP DISCUSSION:

1. Do you share your biggest sorrows and cry to God? When? Where?

2. Have you ever learned a lesson from your pain? Can you share the story?

Activity: cut white squares from plain cotton cloth, like a hankie. Take pens and write out Isaiah 25:8, and/or Psalm 126:5. Place these "tissues" from Jesus in your Bible. Next time you have sorrow, remember that you are not alone in your sadness.

# 12
## Crumbs

Where do crumbs come from? Bread maybe? Daily bread? The bread of life? If there are crumbs in your purse, then there must have been a piece of bread. I hope you ate it! Do you eat the whole piece each day, and get full, or are you just eating crumbs? You know which one nourishes. The word of God, a relationship with Jesus, that is what fills.

Give us this day, our daily bread. — Matthew 6:11

Man shall not live by bread alone, but by every word of God. — Luke 4:4

I am the bread of life ... — John 6:35

I am the living bread ... if any man eat of this bread, he shall live forever ... — John 6:51

Do we crave this bread? We should. We should have a hunger for it every day. This bread gives life and gives it abundantly. It satisfies. When we are hungry, we want something to fill us. When we are empty, there is an uncomfortable void. How do we fill it? We eat!

...it is my Father who gives you the true bread from heaven. For the bread of God is the bread that comes down from heaven and gives life to the world. — John 6:32-33

This is one bread without carbs! Gobble up! Take as much Bread of Life as you want!

## GROUP DISCUSSION:

1. Do you have an unsatisfied soul? What are you craving? What will help?

2. Are you nourished with bread of life crumbs, or stale crumbs from some other "food" that you are ingesting? You are what you eat! Think of God as whole-grain. Anything else is white bread, stripped of all nutrients.

3. When is your best time to read the Word of God? What do you find that helps you make time for the Word, and what helps your mind retain it?

# *"Son" Glasses*

Have you ever tried to look directly at the sun? It's blinding. If we're going to be in the presence of the Lord, we'd better have our "son" glasses on because he is one bright light!

The Lord is my light and my salvation ... — Psalm 27:1

Thy word is a Lamp unto my feet, and a light unto my path. — Psalm 119:105 (KJV)

Can you imagine your entire church congregation sitting in their pews on Sunday morning wearing their sunglasses? Tee-hee. We'd look like we were at a Blues Brothers convention. We'd look so "cool." But this is an analogy about a purse, and who doesn't have sunglasses in theirs?

I like the verse in Isaiah 60:1 that says, "Arise, shine; for thy light is come, and the glory of the Lord is risen upon thee." I'd love to "shine" every morning. "God is light ..." *(1 John 1:5)*. I reflect the light. And light is so much better than darkness.

... the true Light ... gives light to every man that comes into the world. — John 1:9

When you get up in the middle of the night and go into your kitchen to get a drink of water or a snack, you turn on the light. Why? Because you want to see. Things are so much clearer in the light. I encourage you to use your "Son" glasses every day, or night.

## GROUP DISCUSSION:

1. Share how God has shed His light on you.

2. Has He ever revealed the devil's deception over a particular area of your life?

3. Do you make decisions in God's light? Name some big ones that should never be done without His approval. How about small ones? He cares about those too.


Have fun with this. I can hear you giggling already.

Activity: Everyone put on your sunglasses. As a group, say over and over, "God is light! He illuminates!"

# 14
## Cell Phone

A cell phone from Jesus, woo-hoo! No fees, no wrong numbers, no solicitors, no minutes, no butt dials - just a direct line to Christ when you need to talk to him. Prayer, of course, is our cell phone. All throughout the Bible, the saints talked to the Lord through conversation. When you pray alone, think of speaking to Christ like you're on the phone. You talk, then listen. You talk, then listen. When you listen, you will hear Him urging you, speaking truths, encouraging, loving, giving wisdom, scolding and so much more. But to hear him, sometimes you must be quiet. There is so much noise in the world. I suffer from noise anxiety and must go away sometimes just to have silence.

My favorite verse in the Bible is Psalm 46:10, "Be still and know that I am God." He is not always a roaring lion. This verse makes believing so simple. He can come as silent as a whisper.

How often are we listening? How often do you actually sit still for one whole minute? I challenge you to try it. You will be amazed. Then, sit and silence your mind for an entire minute. It's even harder to do, nearly impossible!

"Hear me when I call, O God ..." (Psalm 4:1). Love that verse too. It's perfect for this illustration.

Ring, ring.

Hello? Jesus? Can you talk?

I imagine him saying, "Yes, daughter. What's on your mind?"

Oh my gosh! Someone who actually listens to me? Wonderful!

As for me, I will call upon God; and the Lord shall save me. Evening, and morning and at noon, I will pray and cry aloud, and he shall hear my voice.
— Psalm 55:16-17

Be anxious for nothing; but in everything by prayer and supplication with thanksgiving let your requests be made known unto God. — Philippians 4:6

So "call" Him. What's stopping you? Remember to pray to the Lord each and every time you reach for your cell phone. Especially if you're driving!

## GROUP DISCUSSION:

1. If you can't hear him talking to you, there's a cell phone tower down. Thing is, he never hangs up, so if there is a communication break-down, it's you. What can you do about it?

Activity: Sit and be still for 60 seconds. Be absolutely QUIET!!!! Ask God to talk to you, then just listen ...

# 15
## Keys

How many keys do you have? Earthly keys are heavy, noisy, easy to lose and a nuisance to carry. Kingdom keys, however, are glorious. Inside your handbag from Christ, there is a set of keys just waiting for you to use them to open doors of opportunity.

> Behold, I stand at the door and knock; if any man hear my voice and open the door, I will come in and eat with him and they with me. — Revelation 3:20

What doors can He open for you if you have the keys to His kingdom? Here are a few suggestions: love, forgiveness, travel, work opportunities, better health, new friends, evangelism, peace of mind, fruits of the spirit (Galatians 5:22), eternal life.

Here's a fun activity. Count the keys on your key ring right now. Try to come up with that many uses for kingdom keys. See what happens.

> Open to me the gates of righteousness...This gate of the Lord, into which the righteous shall enter .... — Psalm 118:19-20

First and foremost, open the door to Christ. Then use His keys to open more doors to a richer life, and help others open doors as well.

## GROUP DISCUSSION:

1. What doors has He opened for you?

2. Do the activity mentioned in this section. How many areas of life can be opened with these keys?

3. Keep in mind that God may not give you the keys to fame and fortune. He knows what's best and He has a plan for you. Read Jeremiah 29:11.

# 16
## Hand Cream

My hands are so dry from all the work I do. I must remember to moisturize often. That's why there's hand cream in our bags. When we put forth our hands to work in God's service, we must care for them just as well. The Proverbs 31 woman worked with her hands. She wove cloth, gathered food, made meals, worked in the garden, helped the poor, made clothing, sold clothing, and served her family. Whew, busy gal! But does that sound so different from what we do now? Not much has changed for women. We do it all!

Give her the fruit of her hands and let her own works praise her in the gates. — Proverbs 31:31

Let us rise up and build. So they strengthened their hands for this good work. — Nehemiah 2:18

Establish the work of our hands for us ... — Psalm 90:17

We are called for service. We are all part of the body of Christ and we each have a role to play. You cannot be the wart on the finger that just sits there and serves no purpose. We use our hands to pray, to hold our Bibles, to comfort those in need, to make a phone call, to cook a meal, to help when a hand is needed, to work for Christ. Do you have a ministry? If not, someone, somewhere needs you. Pray about it. Ask God to show you where He needs you most. Take care of your hands, but use them.

## GROUP DISCUSSION:

1. If you take care of yourself, then you can take care of others. What have you done to take care of yourself this week?

2. Have you worked with your hands this week, or served in a ministry? What did you do?

3. Name some ministries in your church or community where you can get involved.

Leader idea: Ask a local make-up representative for samples of hand cream to pass out to everyone.

# Debit Card – What's in Your Wallet?

Last, but certainly not least in our handbag, is a DEBT card. Not debit, debt. Have you ever played Monopoly? Ever gotten a get out of jail free card? Well, Christ offers us something even better. How about a GET OUT OF HELL FREE card? Don't leave earth without it!

One of the definitions of the word debt is: An offense requiring forgiveness or reparation; sin, trespass. Hmmm. And forgive us our trespasses...sound familiar? When Christ died on the cross for our sins, He paid that debt for us. He died so we could be forgiven and go to heaven. All it takes is our belief in Him.

We are all familiar with John 3:16, but it bears repeating in this context.

> For God so loved the world that he gave his one and only Son, that whoever believes in him shall not perish but have eternal life.

And Romans 5:8 puts it so simply: Christ died for us... Hallelujah! Praise the Lord! Amen!

Don't you want to go to heaven and join the masses of fellow Christians? What a happy alternative to an eternity in fire. I once went to a Beth Moore convention in Birmingham. As I watched from the nose-bleed section, I marveled at the thousands of people who were in the auditorium. Marveled! And that was just a drop in the bucket compared to the millions who will worship with us in New Jerusalem. Sign me up Lord, I want to be there!

He paid our debt. This "Debt" card is in our purse as a reminder and a token. When we use it, let us remember this awesome free gift. Will you use yours by believing that He died for your sins?

Honestly ladies, this is the most important transaction you will ever make in your life.

## Group Discussion:

1. Is there anything in our lives keeping us from feeling like we don't deserve forgiveness, grace, or salvation?

2. Define "whosoever."

3. Remember, His blood cures everything. You don't have to get clean first. He will cleanse you! This is a come as you are invitation!!!

Activity: Make a "Debt Card" using John 3:16. Keep it in your wallet.

# *Conclusion*

When you are saved, you are equipped by Christ with all that you need. This Bible study is simply a fun way to keep Christ in our minds as we go through each day. We women have busy lives and awesome responsibilities, but it is imperative that we not forget who we are and why we are here. We are here because we are His. Each time you use your foundation, lipstick, cell phone, keys and debit card, be reminded of these verses. Everything in your handbag from God has significance. My prayer is that these items will deepen your walk, your faith, your relationship with Him. Be reminded of His love, His help, His good plans for you. Sisters in Christ, be blessed.

www.ingramcontent.com/pod-product-compliance
Lightning Source LLC
Chambersburg PA
CBHW030309030426
42337CB00012B/653